GHOST STORIES
OF
OCEAN CITY, NJ

Ghost Stories
of
Ocean City, NJ

by Tim Reeser

www.ghosttour.com
Ghost <u>Tour</u> of Ocean City, NJ

A candlelight walking tour where fun in the sun turns to fear in the dark! Join us for this fun and entertaining candlelight tour along the avenues of Ocean City's historic town center. Listen to haunting tales of love and loss...legends and shipwrecks...and spirits that roam the night!

From May to October the tour materializes at 8:00 pm outside Central Emporium located at 9th Street & Central Avenue. Tickets can be purchased at tour time.

609-814-0199   www.ghosttour.com

GHOST STORIES OF OCEAN CITY, NJ

1stSight Press
Box 42 Monocacy, PA 19542

Second Printing 2003
Printed in the United States of America
ISBN: 0-9729265-0

To Alanna, who knows all about hunting for spirits in Ocean City

GHOST STORIES
OF
OCEAN CITY, NJ

Contents

GHOST STORIES

of

OCEAN CITY, NJ

Many thanks to my loving wife,
Eileen Mary Brennan, for her help, support
and patience in collecting and researching
the stories within this book. Her enthusiasm,
encouragement and superb storytelling skills
were paramount to moving forward the literary
process and keeping it on track.

*May she always have the sun shining on
her blanket and sand between her toes.*

GHOST STORIES OF OCEAN CITY, NJ

Ocean City is a wonderful summertime beach community where the proverbial *fun in the sun* adage comes true. A memory-indulging boardwalk of summer delights accentuates nature's gift of fine sandy beach and playful ocean surf stretching for miles of picture perfect sunny pleasure. Quaint and varied downtown shopping and an assortment of restaurants extend to the large back bay of boating and fishing abundance. A daytime playland unspoiled by creatures of the night...those ghosts and spirits from the past that elicit *fear in the dark*.

Yes, from ocean to bay and inlet to inlet, Ocean City abounds with tales of the supernatural. This refined island resort, overflowing with summer homes and cottages, certainly has some interesting and extraordinary tales to tell. Stories of a lover's loss and her eternal wait, of visitors who return from the dead and refuse to leave, of mysterious legends that have haunted the island for centuries, and of spirits that roam the island as if they have never left...

UNDER THIS TREE
(THEN GROWING NEAR NORTH STREET)
REV. EZRA B. LAKE   REV. S. WESLEY LAKE
REV. JAMES E. LAKE   REV. WM. H. BURRELL
WITH A PRAYER TO GOD DEDICATED THIS ISLAND
AS A CHRISTIAN SEASIDE RESORT
SEPTEMBER 10, 1879

HON. SIMON LAKE AND REV. WM. B. WOOD
JOINED THEM IN INCORPORATING
THE OCEAN CITY ASSOCIATION
OCTOBER 20, 1879

GHOST STORIES OF OCEAN CITY, NJ

Ocean City is a wonderful summertime beach community where the proverbial *fun in the sun* adage comes true. A memory-indulging boardwalk of summer delights accentuates nature's gift of fine sandy beach and playful ocean surf stretching for miles of picture perfect sunny pleasure. Quaint and varied downtown shopping and an assortment of restaurants extend to the large back bay of boating and fishing abundance. A daytime playland unspoiled by creatures of the night...those ghosts and spirits from the past that elicit *fear in the dark.*

Yes, from ocean to bay and inlet to inlet, Ocean City abounds with tales of the supernatural. This refined island resort, overflowing with summer homes and cottages, certainly has some interesting and extraordinary tales to tell. Stories of a lover's loss and her eternal wait, of visitors who return from the dead and refuse to leave, of mysterious legends that have haunted the island for centuries, and of spirits that roam the island as if they have never left...

UNDER THIS TREE
(THEN GROWING NEAR NORTH STREET)
Rev. EZRA B. LAKE   Rev. S. WESLEY LAKE
Rev. JAMES E. LAKE   Rev. WM. H. BURRELL
WITH A PRAYER TO GOD DEDICATED THIS ISLAND
AS A CHRISTIAN SEASIDE RESORT
SEPTEMBER 10, 1879

HON. SIMON LAKE AND Rev. WM. B. WOOD
JOINED THEM IN INCORPORATING
THE OCEAN CITY ASSOCIATION
OCTOBER 20, 1879

The Founding Father

If we were to anoint someone as the *founding father* of Ocean City as we know it today, perhaps the one individual most worthy of that designation would be Simon Lake. And although he perished in 1881, there are those who believe that Simon can still be seen strolling the Tabernacle grounds, as he did so long ago, when only the vision of a beautiful seaside resort existed.

It all started in September of 1879, when four Methodist clergymen, the three brothers, Wesley, Ezra and James Lake along with William Burrell, crossed the Great Egg Harbor bay to the sparsely populated island of Peck's Beach. They followed a winding cow path to a spot next to a small cedar tree (the remnants of which are said to still exist, memorialized on the Tabernacle grounds). At that tree, the small group of visionaries committed to a dream to which they aspired. To build a Christian resort that would provide sanctuary and healthful recreation for the faithful - an environment that would conform to their Methodist ethic. On that late summer day, they made the decision to pursue a goal that eventually grew to become Ocean City, "America's Greatest Family Resort." Of course, like countless dreams, it would take many years and large amounts of money to accomplish.

Following their return to the mainland, the brothers visited their father, Simon Lake, at his farm in Pleasantville. They convinced him to fund the venture, which he did by borrowing $10,000 against the farm, a considerable risk and a

> dolphin: In classical mythology, a carrier of the souls of the dead to the afterlife world. In Christian myth, the dolphin represents resurrection and salvation, and also represents the Christian Church being guided by Christ.

considerable amount of money in those days. The Lakes used the money to fund the purchase of every square inch of the island for an amount estimated at $100,000. They wanted complete control over the development of the new resort and planned a buyout of all claims, thus avoiding any dissension from problem landowners. The Lake brothers succeeded in their acquisition plan, which was made possible by the money and guidance they received from their father.

Simon Lake became a central figure in the development of the new seaside resort. He served for several years as

president of the Ocean City Association, formed that same year of 1879, to oversee the buying and selling of lots on the island. By all accounts, their new venture proved successful from the very beginning, as they sold more than 500 lots during the first year of operation.

> Original restrictions in the Ocean City Association Deed Form:
> ...that no spirituous, malt, intoxicating or vinous liquors, preparations, or substances... shall be...bought, sold, or kept for sale...and...shall not at any time...erect or setup...any building to be used as a house of prostitution, bawdy-house or house of ill-fame, or dance or gambling house...

The Association reserved the area between 5th and 6th Streets from the bay to the ocean for religious worship. The area became known as the Tabernacle, and by 1881, a large structure existed there as a center of worship. The grounds of the Tabernacle were planted with beautiful gardens and lawns, and Simon Lake could often be seen sitting on the porch of his son's house on 6th Street or wandering among the lovely gardens admiring their beauty.

However, Simon met with a fatal accident very near his beloved Tabernacle. While cutting and clearing brush near the beach, experimenting with conserving the sand dunes, his ax slipped and severed his foot. An infection set in, and back in a time when the miracle of antibiotics did not exist, he died of blood poisoning. The loss shocked the small town, still in its formative stage. The town patriarch was gone and deeply missed by his sons and the community.

The Ocean City Association memorialized the tragic and unexpected demise of Simon Lake with a passage in the minutes of a December 1881 meeting:

> "Whereas, the Honorable Simon Lake...has by a mysterious providence been removed from this life, as we trust to a holier and happier state...we are profoundly affected and...have sustained an irreparable loss..."

Our story now switches to the present. A notable Ocean City resident and business owner, well-known for his knowledge of the island's history and his expertise on the early architectural styles of its buildings, surmises that perhaps Simon Lake's ghost haunts the Tabernacle grounds. He based his theory on multiple sightings of an apparition seen wandering those grounds and the circumstances under which he emerges. The specter of an old man appears leisurely strolling among the gardens, admiring the grounds, just as Simon did so many years ago. He is usually spotted in the midst of community upheaval over an unusually contentious issue. He appeared wandering the Tabernacle grounds several years back during the highly publicized referendum to reconsider legalizing the sale of alcohol and materialized again more recently after ratification of a new city high school.

Could it be, that Simon Lake, Ocean City's *founding father*, taken from this life under "mysterious providence" perhaps before his time, before he had the chance to complete his work here in Ocean City...the father who backed his sons' venture and guided them in the early years...Is it possible that Simon Lake to this day watches over the City...guiding her as he did then...as any *father* would?

"Emily" by Tony Troy

The original painting, shown here, was considered too "scary" by the staff at the Flanders Hotel, resulting in the more elegant picture that exists there today.

EMILY

Standing like a sentinel on the beach, the Flanders Hotel continues to serve as one of Ocean City's best-known resort hotels. The interior, adorned with glittering chandeliers, oriental design carpets and life-size murals, exudes an old world charm of elegance and sophistication. After many years of decline and several attempts to convert this magnificent building to something other than a hotel, recent renovations have restored its former glory, and it survives, perched proudly on the Boardwalk at 11th Street, as the "grand old lady" of Ocean City. And, like any "grand old lady," the stories she can tell...of elegant misty forms...of closets harboring secrets...of ominous, subterranean catacombs...are memories of long ago intertwined with haunting tales of today.

The name Flanders traces back to a tragic time in the world's history - World War I, the "War to End All Wars." Considered the first "modern war," it became the largest conflict up to that time in history - measured in the number of countries involved and lives lost. New technologies such as airplanes, tanks, submarines and poisonous gas, contributed to killing on a massive scale.

Many thousands of lives were lost by both sides in battles fought in trenches for control of relatively small parcels of land. One of these memorable battles took place in Belgium, in an area known as Flanders.

The hotel opened in 1923, just a few years after the war ended. And with memories still fresh and emotions still raw, the owners chose the name Flanders to commemorate the battle - a battle immortalized in a haunting poem written by a member of the Canadian medical corps, Lieutenant Colonel John McCrae.

Affected deeply by the agony and suffering he witnessed on the battlefields at Flanders, and particularly by the death of a close friend there, he penned the eerily touching epic ballad "In Flanders Fields." The poem pays tribute to those who lost their lives in the horrific battle and also reminds future generations not to forget the soldiers' struggle...or, as the poem so poignantly suggests, they will return from the dead...to haunt us forever.

"IN FLANDERS FIELDS"

In Flanders Fields the poppies blow
  Between the crosses, row on row,
That mark our place; and in the sky
The Larks, still bravely singing, fly
Scarce heard amid the guns below.

We are the Dead. Short days ago
We lived, felt dawn, saw sunset glow,
Loved, and were loved, and now we lie
  In Flanders Fields.

Take up our quarrel with the foe:
To you from failing hands we throw
The torch; be yours to hold it high.
  If ye break faith with us who die
We shall not sleep, though poppies grow
  In Flanders Fields.

Today, a step into the Flanders *is* like taking a step back in time, to the grandiose days of the 1920's – stately

ballrooms, grand hallways - and perhaps, if the stories can be believed, it is also a step into a place where ghosts appear and a phantom roams about.

The most notable sighting appears in the form of an elegant looking young lady called Emily. Many reports and numerous accounts exist of the lovely maiden dressed in a wedding gown. A recent wedding reception held in the ballroom known as the Boardroom is typical of Emily's intrusions. As the wedding photographer choreographed the attendees about the room, the new bride experienced a weird feeling, as if an unseen presence had joined their party. Sure enough, when the wedding pictures were developed, a distinct, puffy, billowing cloud-like mass appeared on one. Convinced that the photographer had

captured an image of Emily in the photograph, she sent the picture to the Flanders, where it resides for public viewing in the foyer. Several spectacular wall murals by local artist Tony Troy also decorate the foyer. Purportedly based on eyewitness descriptions of Emily, the paintings show a beautiful young lady in a long white dress in a dream-like scene.

Emily captured on film at a High School prom held at the Flanders?

Emily manifests in other ways as well. Mysterious melodies emanating from the piano, rearranged settings in the banquet room and frequent sightings of a ghostly figure are almost exclusively attributed to Emily. Guests and employees spot her throughout the hotel, but mostly Emily appears in the lobby area, the hallways and the banquet rooms on the second floor.

Kathy and Maria, employees at the Flanders, have no doubt that the old hotel is haunted, and they have a slew of stories to share. "You can tell when Emily is present. It's an eerie feeling, as if the blood is draining from your body, and then you get icy cold, and your hairs stand up on end!"

While attending an employee meeting in the Crystal Room, a second floor banquet room, Kathy recalled a time when they heard banging and rattling coming from one of the closets. The doorknob turned and the door shook as if someone was trying to get out. Upon opening the door, nobody was inside, and according to Kathy, "There wasn't even a knob on the inside of the closet...it was turning on its own!"

Another time, from the hallway known as the Hall of Mirrors, Maria heard someone playing the piano in the Crystal Room. As she entered the room, she expected to find children fooling around with the grand piano, but a ghostly realization overcame her as the playing stopped...and again, no one was there!

Emily also seems to have a playful, mischievous side that Maria admits is a nuisance that they have learned to live with. Emily's antics usually occur when the staff prepares for a banquet or wedding reception. They find table settings disrupted - missing salt and pepper shakers, silverware rearranged and dishes neatly stacked in their storage location after having been set out on the tables.

Other employees report encounters with Emily elsewhere in the old hotel. The maintenance man once met Emily in the basement, a lonely area of mazed hallways and secret passages - a place they call the catacombs. He saw Emily crouched down looking through some boxes. She looked up at him...turned, walked down the hall...and disappeared.

Sightings by guests also contribute to the mystery. A young boy told his mother about the conversation he had with a nice lady and

The Hall of Mirrors, also known as "Peacock Alley"

then led her into the Hall of Mirrors to point her out. He pointed to an empty wall and said, "There she is!" His mother saw no one. But then, as they were leaving, the boy saw the painting of Emily on the foyer wall and said, "Look mommy, that's the lady I was talking to!"

Roberta, a magazine photographer, related a curious encounter she had outside the Flanders Hotel where the boardwalk descends to street level. It happened on the day before Christmas while visiting her mother in Ocean City over the holiday. Roberta headed to the beach to capture an early morning picture of the sun rising over the ocean.

As Roberta walked up the ramp, she noticed a white mass near the corner where the restaurant sits. At first, she thought it was steam from a vent but no vent existed. As she approached, the mist moved away, and realizing the oddity of it, she stopped. The mist also stopped. She again walked toward it and again it moved away. She stopped again. It stopped again. On her third approach, the mist disappeared - vanished completely. After hearing the stories of Emily and recalling that extensive renovations were being made to the Flanders at the time, Roberta thought that perhaps all of the activity inside caused

Emily to venture outside, resulting in their chance meeting.

However, the most frequent sightings of Emily occur near the piano on the second floor where John McCrae's poem is prominently displayed. Because the poem laments the fate of fallen soldiers, some people surmise that perhaps Emily lost her lover in a war and awaits his return.

Others say that maybe Emily has returned from the afterlife in search of a ring she lost while a guest or as an employee. A report exists of a young woman, an employee at one time, who hung herself in the girls' dormitory that stands in the parking lot next to the hotel. Could this be the source of the sightings of the mysterious phantom of the Flanders Hotel? Has she returned looking for something she left behind or lost inside? There is no way to know.

Whether Emily is looking for a lost ring or is waiting for her lover to return, those who enter this grand hotel should listen for her song and watch for her misty form as she roams about searching and waiting...

Penland Place, now JJ's Asbury Cafe

Uncle Lou

Uncle Lou is an extraordinary friend. No matter that Uncle Lou departed from this world years ago, he still helps his earthly friend, Jim Penland. Whenever Jim talks about his property at the corner of Asbury Avenue and 7th Street, the topic of Uncle Lou, "The Finder of Lost Things," is sure to come up. A friend to Jim while he lived, Uncle Lou continues to reach out to Jim as a friend, even after passing to the other side.

Jim's one-of-kind building sparkles with personality. The ornately detailed, eccentrically painted exterior features a distinctive, three-story conical tower, all marvelously colored in pink, yellow and blue. This attention-grabbing structure, so reminiscent of an earlier era, creates an image that proclaims, "This place is haunted! Anything that looks like this has to be!" And so it is!

A new tenant recently moved into the first floor and opened JJ's Asbury Café, a steak and seafood restaurant. The exterior sports a fresh coat of paint in a new color combination, and the interior renovations make for a pleasant dining atmosphere. However, the building has a history...and the history is what adds that something extra special to this very unique place.

Situated in Ocean City's original commercial district, the peculiar looking building dates back to well over 100 years ago. At one time or another, it housed a dairy store, a church, a tackle shop and an antique store. Jim acquired the rundown property about 40 years ago and renovated the entire building. The distinguishing tower no longer existed, but he found the original construction blueprints and rebuilt the sphere to the exact design and dimensions. The tower served as a crowning reminder to the passing

shoppers to come in and browse Jim's unique gift shop contained within.

An interesting item turned up when Jim began renovating the inside. Tucked behind a wall he found an old dairy store container filled with hair curls and needles and thread. According to Jim the container held Victorian-era "mourning

"Hair is at once the most delicate and lasting of our materials, and survives us, like love. It is so light, so gentle, so escaping from the idea of death, that with a lock of hair belonging to a child or friend, we may almost look up to heaven and compare notes with the angelic nature - may almost say, "I have a piece of thee here, not unworthy of thy being now."
-Leigh Hunt, May, 1855
Godey's Lady's Book

curls" used for comforting those mourning the loss of a loved one. He marks this find as the beginning of the supernatural activity that continues to this day. It is as though disturbing the curls awakened the spirits to haunt the old building. Everyone who has occupied the building since has experienced some type of paranormal activity.

When Jim had his gift shop there, store items moved on their own, pictures fell off the wall and music boxes mysteriously played their tunes. Many times while Jim and store manager Les discussed a particular piece of merchandise, it suddenly moved. When referring to one of the many pictures hanging on the walls, it might have suddenly fallen to the floor. Jim talked of his most bizarre experience: "It was the Christmas season, and we had these wonderful windup music boxes for sale. It was almost quitting time, when all of a sudden, seven of these music boxes began playing! Of course it was impossible because I was the only one in the place!" But the melodies from the music boxes made him think of Uncle Lou.

At the time, Jim's dear friend, Louis J. Martin, Uncle Lou to him, lay terminally ill in a hospital. Jim's visits with Uncle Lou were becoming more and more distressing as he became less and less responsive. Remembering that Uncle Lou at one time performed as a singer and that he loved opera, Jim decided to bring along one of the music boxes on his next visit. As Jim relates, "When I opened the box and the music started to play, Uncle Lou heard it and let me know that he knew I was there." Shortly thereafter, Uncle Lou passed away, and Jim is convinced that the music box helped him say goodbye to his best friend.

Uncle Lou

After Uncle Lou died, Jim often thought about his good friend. Eventually he noticed that each time he lost something around the shop... a missing tool, a misplaced notepad...if he asked Uncle Lou to help him find what he had lost, it would turn up. The other employees took to doing the same thing, and it worked for them as well. This led to calling Uncle Lou the *"Finder of Lost Things,"* and even today, Jim will call on Uncle Lou for help if he has trouble finding something.

The weird activity in Jim's building continues unabated as confirmed by the new tenants. While converting the interior for use as a restaurant, several people heard thumping and footsteps on the second floor. They knew no one could be up there, since the steps leading to the second floor were removed years ago. John, one of the owners, and his partner became curious one night when the noises persisted and climbed a ladder to the second floor to check it out. As they stood looking around the unused space abandoned to the dust and cobwebs, they suddenly heard banging on the glass window coming from the outside. John's partner hurried down the ladder claiming, "I've seen enough! Let's get out of here."

On another occasion, a week or so before their grand opening, John remained behind alone in the building after showing family and friends around the new restaurant. Hearing noise upstairs, he again climbed a ladder, and as he poked his head up through the hole in the floor, a big piece of plywood nailed over a window crashed to the floor. Thoroughly spooked, he locked up and left. After which he commented, "I don't like to be alone in here!"

In the past, Jim tried several times to make contact with the spirits inhabiting the old corner store. Visits from mediums to "read" the building indicate that multiple spirits occupy the property, and a number of séances revealed a strong presence dwells within the structure. A "witch" from New York performed her magic on the place and concluded that the building is "situated" in such a way that it could possibly be a portal to the spirit world.

So did the discovery of the mourning curls open the old building in the center of town to the spirit world? Or were the spirits just as active before Jim got there? His attempts to communicate with them have revealed their presence, but who they might be, or what

The mourning curls and box found hidden in the wall.

they might want is uncertain. Perhaps someday the mystery will be solved.

For now, Jim is certain that Uncle Lou haunts the old building at 660 Asbury Avenue, and he is also certain that Uncle Lou continues to be a good friend, helping him when he needs it.

The Milabelle

A "*guesthouse where they might check out but <u>they</u> never leave*" (to paraphrase a song by the *Eagles*) is perhaps the best way to describe the building located in the 1100 block of Central Avenue, where it seems the ghost of a phantom cat roams about and guests from the past refuse to check out.

The Milabelle functioned at one time as a guesthouse but now serves as a comfortable single-family home to Jeanne and Dave Swift. But the house is no ordinary home. Owned over the years by a string of widowed women, stories of ghostly visitors and strange poltergeist-like activity occur frequently enough to make this one of the more paranormally active buildings on the island.

Jeanne is an avid Ocean City history buff, which led her to trace the house's ancestry from old tax and deed records. She discovered that it dates back to the very beginning of the island's conversion to a seaside resort by the Lake brothers. Built in the 1890's, the first owner, a Mrs. Asher, became widowed during its construction, and the property deeds further indicate that several subsequent owners were also widows, some of whom were widowed while living in the house. Eventually, the rambling home converted to a guesthouse and functioned during the 1950's and 60's as the "Milabelle Guest House."

> "No Cat Calling from the Porch" This cryptic command appeared along with the check-in and check-out times and other instructions on the back of the door to the rooms in the Milabelle when it functioned as a guesthouse.

When the Swifts acquired the house, it suffered from years of neglect, causing Jeanne to describe the rundown condition of the place as eerily resembling the "Addam's Family" house. They spent much of their time repairing and painting the exterior and updating and renovating the interior rooms. Interestingly enough, one of the theories concerning ghostly encounters centers on the renovation of old houses. Reports of supernatural activity increase when affected houses are rehabilitated. Perhaps the hammering and pounding or the rearranging of walls and doors provides the catalyst to awaken the spirits, causing increased paranormal activity. Uncertain whether the renovations enlivened the spirits or the periodic appearance of vanishing visitors is the norm for their house, the unusual phenomena continues, even if the Swifts are somewhat accustomed to it by now.

Through Jeanne's research, a plausible explanation may exist for at least one otherworldly visitor. Jeanne described a dream she had after dozing off in the parlor following a hard day of work on the house...a dream she knew had something to do with a previous owner. She dreamt of a man with thick dark hair, a red complexion and dressed as if from the early 1900's...in a long brown coat and boots... wandering around the house inspecting the latest renovations. In the background, Jeanne could hear a woman's voice calling Charles...Charles." Later on, when searching the tax records, Jeanne discovered that a man named Charles bought the house in 1927, and he lived there with his wife,

Visitors from the past are seen here.

Matilda. It so happens that shortly after acquiring the house, Charles passed away, and Matilda became another of the widowed owners of the house. Jeanne feels that Charles visited their newly renovated home to inspect the changes made to the house in which he once lived. She sensed his approval of the alterations and his contentment that the house once again had someone devoted to its care and preservation.

Jeanne had another weird experience also in the parlor. She again fell asleep after an exhausting day painting and fixing up. As she slowly emerged from that fuzzy state between sleep and consciousness, Jeanne felt a touch on her cheek. She remembers thinking that Dave came into the room and kissed her because the pressure on her cheek felt so real. But as Jeanne fully woke up, she realized Dave would not be home from work for several more hours, and the kids were outside playing. Jeanne lay there completely alone.

Several supernatural encounters have occurred in the library. Many times the door has latched from the inside - when nobody is in the room. And their children have had a few unsettling episodes there as well. One time, their son entered the library where a man dressed in a suit, wearing a derby and carrying a suitcase, appeared. The man looked up in surprise, and then disappeared. On another occasion, Dave discovered his son sitting on the carpet in the middle of the night, picking at the fringe. Dave asked him what he was doing, and he replied, "They told me to do this." As Dave led him back to bed, he suddenly heard a woman's voice in a sarcastic tone state, "Where are you going, sweetie?"

The next morning when they asked their son why he was in the library, he said, "*They* were talking to me. The lady likes me, but she said she can't eat anymore, her throat hurts." His description of her closely matched that of a former owner named Virginia, who found it difficult to part with the house and eventually died from throat cancer.

> Old Hag: [Encounters] vary, but some are common to most incidents. The victim awakes...feeling an invisible weight pressing on the chest...Some Old Hag attacks begin with sounds of phantom footsteps approaching...
> -Ancient Folklore

Likewise, both Jeanne and Dave have seen a white, misty, female-like form in other areas of their home. Early one morning while still in bed, Dave felt a tingling sensation run through his body, and as the bedroom door opened, an ethereal figure glided over to the window and paused as if looking out...and then suddenly vanished. A similar ectoplasmic shape startled Jeanne one evening as it came toward her while she sat on the couch (the same couch where she experienced the phantom kiss). As the fog-like form approached her it just kept going...right through her...into the other room.

A few truly scary and very real mishaps have occurred over the years involving the roof of the house. Repairing a second story leak, Dave worked from a ladder that was placed against the outside wall and tied securely to the building. Suddenly, the rope snapped; Dave fell with the sliding ladder, crashed onto the porch roof and tumbled to the ground. Luckily, his injuries were not severe, and after a brief visit to the hospital, he recovered quickly. Jeanne often ponders whether Dave survived the fall miraculously unscathed

> silkies: Female spirits, dressed in rustling silk... perform household chores and are valued by people living in large houses. But silkies can be perverse, too: a house that is tidy might be left disarranged, and a messy house might be put in order. A silky also can act as the guardian of a house...
> -Scottish Folklore

due to a "guardian angel widow" watching over him that day.

However, it appears that the guardian-widow's protection does not extend beyond the Swift's Central Avenue house. Shortly after Dave's accident, a roofer friend agreed to help Dave fix the problematic roof. That same night, after a day spent working on the roof, their friend, a relatively young man- only in his 30's, dropped dead of a heart attack. Whether there may actually be some sinister connection to Dave's accident, the Swifts remain wary of the rooftop.

And there may be a secret on the third floor lurking in what once was Room 7 of the old guesthouse. For a long time, their dog would not enter this room. If they tried carrying him in, the dog would cry and whimper and escape the room as soon as possible. Eventually overcoming his fear - to a small degree anyway – the dog took to dashing into the room where he would cower under the bed. Today, the dog still avoids the room and seldom ventures there.

But their cats have adopted Room 7 as their own private sanctuary. From the very beginning, it became the cats' favorite place, and they seldom venture far from the room. Is there something strange about Room 7 that would scare the dog as it does? Better yet, is there something even stranger that would attract the cats? In the folklore of many countries around the world, cats are thought to have a connection to the spirit world...maybe that explains the unusual behaviour of the animals. Certainly, Room 7 ranks as one of the odder places in the Central Avenue home.

Room 7

Perhaps the most extraordinary sightings involve what the Swift's call the "ghost cat." On numerous occasions, almost every member of the family has encountered this netherworld cat, from glimpses of its misty form to actual contact with the feline ghost. Jeanne felt the cat lying on her chest as she woke up one morning only to see it vanish as it jumped from the bed. The illusory pet awakened Dave while he too slept, and the kids frequently glimpse its disappearing shape as it rounds the corner of a room or hall.

Jeanne is convinced she knows the origin of the "ghost cat" and the reason it still frolics through their home. Several years ago, she found a cat outside the house gasping its last breath. Thinking that the poor thing may

Cats of the Milabelle

have been hit by a car or ingested poisoned food and hoping to revive it, Jeanne brought the barely conscious cat into the house. Unable to do anything for it, she frantically called a nearby veterinarian friend. The vet tried to save the ailing cat, but as its condition deteriorated and the suffering increased, she mercifully put the cat out of its misery and euthanized it right there in Jeanne's house. Shortly thereafter, Jeanne had her first experience with the "ghost cat"...and encounters persist to this day. She thinks the cat, prematurely killed, continues to search for a way home and thus clambers about their house in its eternal quest for peace.

This exceptional home apparently continues as the Milabelle once did, a place busy with guests...except these guests appear and disappear as they please.

Horror In Ocean City

Compared to modern times, horror took a different form in the old days. The Ocean City Daily newspaper ran these clips during August, 1931:

TUESDAY, AUGUST 4, 1931

THE HORRORSCOPE
WRITTEN BY ONE WHO KNOWS ALL; SEES ALL
*   *   *

Persons Born On This Day Should Avoid Loose
Planks In the Boardwalk

FRIDAY, AUGUST 7, 1931

THE HORRORSCOPE
WRITTEN BY ONE WHO KNOWS ALL; SEES ALL
*   *   *

It will be better today to have horses instead of
mules on the beach. There is no room for them on
the streets, day or night. Where the horse paths
should be, the tourists park their automobiles.

TUESDAY, AUGUST 25, 1931

THE HORRORSCOPE
WRITTEN BY ONE WHO KNOWS ALL; SEES ALL
*   *   *

If Rain Falls Today, Be Careful in Walking Under
the Boardwalk, Lest You Get Wet and Strike Your
Head on Rafters and Be Missing at Mealtime

Mrs. Leeds's 13th Child
From the Oyster Creek Inn
Leeds Point, NJ

The 13th Child

The horrifying legend of Mrs. Leeds' 13th child, cursed at birth and destined to roam the dark lonely Pine Barrens of South Jersey, continues to haunt communities from the seashore to Philadelphia and the cities of North Jersey.

All roads leading into Ocean City from the mainland pass through the Pine Barrens somewhere along the way. Rushing to and from the beach through the stunted and deformed trees, over the small dark streams that feed the jungle-like forest, most of us are unaware of what lies beyond the deserted sandy roads that disappear into the nothingness of the desolate region. In the light of day as we cruise through the sparsely populated corridors formed by scrub pine and scraggly oak, we rarely give a second thought to the tangled and abandoned forest. At night, we follow the narrow tunnel of light formed by our headlights, safe and isolated from the unknown darkness. But according to the legend, among these pine trees and thick undergrowth, along the roadways where development has yet to touch and few people live, hides the creature they call the Jersey Devil, watching as we roll by.

The few scattered inhabitants, traditionally called "pineys," familiar with the Pine Barrens and its ways, are just as familiar with the legend. And many campers have spent a scary night on the edge of civilization in the vast forest, nestled among its branches and sandy barren terrain, ensconced in the pitch-black darkness, where the sounds of screeching animals and galloping hoof beats can be heard that some say are the rampaging 'Devil, the 13th child of Mrs. Leeds.

Stories of the Jersey Devil have existed since the early 1700s and are firmly woven into the folklore of the region. Even before the Europeans arrived, the Native American tribes had a word for the vast area that meant "place of the dragon." The most popular contemporary story places the origin of the 'Devil in the area of Leeds Point, less than 20 miles up the coast from Ocean City.

One legend has it that an itinerant preacher, having failed in his attempt to convert Mrs. Leeds, condemned her unborn child, cursing it as the offspring of Satan himself. Shortly after the delivery, the child suddenly mutated into a beast with a horse's head, large horns, yellow eyes, claws for fingers, a long tail and wings sprouting from its shoulders. Erupting with a bellowing scream, the monster crashed through the cabin window into the darkness beyond.

Another account claims that a hungry gypsy placed a curse on the pregnant Mrs. Leeds after being refused food and lodging at her cabin. She gave birth to a deformed and misshapen baby that spent its entire childhood locked away in the attic until the grotesque creature grew too big and violent to control, escaping into the woods after killing and mutilating local livestock.

> Roaring Bull of Bagbury:
> The Devil, in the form of a ghostly, frightening bull. As a mortal, the bull had been a mean man who had performed only two good deeds...As a ghost, he was doomed to haunt a farm with such loud roars and bellows that the farmer called 12 parsons together to (exorcise) him. The parsons drove the bull to the church where they finally conjured him into a size so small that they could stuff him into a snuffbox. The box was sent to the Red Sea for 1,000 years.
> -English Folklore

In yet another version, the area of Estellville is identified as the birthplace of the Jersey Devil, even closer to Ocean City, just 15 miles away. Sightings in the early 19th century link two famous names to the legend. Joseph Bonaparte, an ex-King of Spain living in exile in New Jersey, reportedly spotted the Jersey Devil while hunting game near his estate. And United States naval hero Commodore Stephen Decatur, while visiting a munitions factory located in the Pine Barrens, fired a cannonball at the creature as it flew overhead, striking it with no ill-effect whatsoever.

Legend has it that Captain Kidd beheaded one of his men to guard his buried treasure forever. The headless pirate and the Jersey Devil became friends, and can be seen in the evenings walking on the beach and nearby marshland!

In January of 1909, the Jersey Devil made newspaper headlines when a creature said to resemble the legendary Leeds Devil appeared in over 30 towns in New Jersey and Pennsylvania during a one-week period. Reportedly spotted by more than 1,000 people, several communities were terrorized to the point of mass hysteria, temporarily shutting down schools and factories. As abruptly as the sightings of the strange creature started, they stopped. The beast was not captured, and the phenomena went unexplained.

Whatever it may be, the legend of the Jersey Devil has remained a constant in the folklore of South Jersey's Pine Barrens for close to 300 years. And if ever you come across Route 666, traveling the deserted back roads near Estellville, perhaps it is best to just keep on going... for the sign of the beast might just foretell the approach of a 'Devil of a different kind.

A ghost story at City Hall

City Hall Specter

As one crosses the bay and enters Ocean City from the 9th Street bridge, traveling through the traffic lights and past restaurants, an imposing landmark looms at the corner of Asbury Avenue. City Hall anchors the center of town. A busy place of municipal government, it is home to the Mayor's office, City Council Chambers and various administrative offices...and possibly...home to a door-rattling ghost from City Hall's past that still haunts the halls and corridors it once served!

Ocean City's forefathers chose the site of City Hall for its conspicuous location, and true to their intent, it stands out as one of the city's most noticeable and notable buildings. The colonnaded exterior design combines Greek and Roman architectural elements creating a grand image of power and authority, a fortress surrounded by downtown storefronts and seashore cottages. Behind the massive walls, elected officials and busy administrators make the decisions and perform the tasks necessary to keep the city government operating.

Constructed in 1914 for the paltry sum of just under $80,000 (including the furnishings), some taxpayers still strongly opposed the newly built structure calling it a

"reckless expenditure." Up until that time, the city government had no real home, and council meetings were held in any available space including the firehouse and several private residences.

> ### Old City Hall
>
> Harry Headley, the mayor when City Hall was built, reportedly held several meetings in the small building he owned that still stands behind City Hall. After the new building was occupied on New Year's Day 1915, they still referred to the Mayor's building as "old city hall."

City Hall contained more than just the local government offices when it opened. The fire and police departments were headquartered there, and a new eight-cell city jail replaced the old two-cell jail house known as the "Naley," a quaint structure named after the first prisoner held there in 1900.

So much for the ordinary. Apparently, nighttime activity goes beyond public meetings and nightly office cleaning. Stories of shuffling footsteps, an erratic elevator, slamming doors and a well-dressed apparition suggest

that something extraordinary roams the darkened corridors of City Hall.

Beth, a member of the public relations department, tells about her supernatural experience, which occurred late one night while working overtime. As the hours ticked by, Beth realized everyone else had left and she remained alone in City Hall. Or so she thought. In the late night quiet, Beth heard the sound of the elevator moving, but when it stopped at her floor and the doors did not open, Beth went to investigate. Thinking that perhaps a mechanical malfunction prevented the door from opening, she pressed the button and the door slid open...to an empty elevator. In Beth's own words, she "freaked a little" and hurried back to her office. Beth really panicked when she again heard the sound of the elevator moving and the sudden slamming of an office door down the hallway. Thoroughly frightened, Beth packed up and rushed down the steps out into the street.

> Harry Headley spent most of his adult life serving Ocean City in one capacity or another. In addition to multiple terms as mayor, he served several terms on city council. Credited with being the driving force behind the construction of the new City Hall, Harry also led the efforts to establish the growing island's fire department, police force and public library.

Beth often received good-natured kidding from her co-workers after sharing her ghostly encounter. Her fellow administrator, Mary Anne, teased Beth about what the ghost would do when it finally got her. That was until Mary Anne had her own encounter late one evening while working after an election. When the elevator started going up and down on its own and office doors started slamming, Mary Anne also left the building in a frightened rush out the door.

Joe, a key administrator at City Hall, has heard the stories over the years and also has had a few strange experiences of his own. One of the more bizarre stories came from the cleaning contractor for City Hall. Joe received a call from the company after an employee of theirs refused to work in the building anymore: "They asked me why I didn't tell them that the building was haunted; I told them I didn't know that it was."

As Joe tells it, City Hall can be a hotbed of activity late into the night with the monthly council meetings, zoning reviews and related sessions. However, most evenings the building is completely deserted except for the personnel hired by the cleaning contractor. Usually, they work late into the evening and number only a handful. Joe told the story as he heard it from the frightened cleaning man: "He was working in the evening on the third floor, around the corner from Chambers. He felt something behind him, turned and saw the ghost of an elderly, well-dressed man, in old-time clothes, bent over with age and his head turned down...never looking up...and as the spirit approached, it kept going, right through him. He left the building and would not return."

Joe has also heard the doors and footsteps on the third floor. "Lots of people claim they've heard doors opening and closing and footsteps on the third floor just outside the Chamber room. I've heard them myself while working late in the evening. My office is on the first floor at the bottom of the staircase. I heard the

distinct sound of a swooshing door – the only door that can make this noise is the double door just outside of

Council Chambers on the third floor. I also heard footsteps, but when I went upstairs, no one was there."

Joe mentioned a time when the subject of ghosts came up at an office get-together held at a local restaurant. It shocked everyone when they learned that they all heard the same unexplained noises. They performed a test by opening and closing various doors. The only door that made the sound they were hearing was the double door to Council Chambers...in the same area the cleaning contractor saw *his* ghost!

Due to the constant changeover in City Hall occupants over the years, elected city officials coming and going, public service departments forming, merging, and moving (at one  time or another the fire company, police department, city jail and telephone company operator were based there), many individuals have dwelled inside the walls of the city government building. This makes speculation difficult on the possible identity of the specter and unexplained phenomena reported there.

But is it perhaps a former mayor who haunts City Hall? George Richards had one day left in his term as Mayor. The next day a newly elected mayor would takeover. On May 21st 1943, George Richards passed away - his last official day in office. Technically, George never completed his term...perhaps he continues riding the elevator and walking the corridors...perhaps he continues with business in Council Chambers and the Mayor's office...perhaps Mayor Richards never wanted to leave office...and perhaps he never has!

Pirate Queens & Buried Treasure

Pirates in Ocean City! Not a legacy typically associated with this idyllic summer resort, but nevertheless true. Pirates and privateers operated unrestrained along the New Jersey coast 300 years ago, using the convenient back bays and coves to hide, make repairs and replenish supplies. And typically, pirates mean treasure...buried treasure. A multitude of rumors and legends concerning buried treasure along the Jersey coast exist, as do legends of the ghosts left behind to guard the booty.

As legends go, there may be some element of fact, but when referring to pirates, legends are built on fear. Fear of their ruthless nature...their cunning ways...their cutthroat tendencies.

Famous pirates like Blackbeard and Captain Kidd were known to sail the Jersey coast, as were the not so well known, like Calico Jack and his "Pirate Queens" – Anne Bonny and Mary Read.

Back in those days, a well-established whaling operation existed on Peck's Beach, present day Ocean City.

Some accounts indicate that pirates referred to the non-descript island as Ocean Towne and were attracted to the accessible bay and convenient location that provided unimpeded views of passing ships that they either hid from or preyed on.

From a 1930s edition of the Ocean City Daily:

"...a band of pirates made their headquarters in Great Egg Harbor Bay...according to old timers...the pirates...landed...on 'Dead Man's Island'...they had a dispute over how to divide the treasure and one of the pirates is...killed. Before leaving...the band buried this luckless man on the island...His ghost is said to roam the lonely spot, on dark nights, restlessly seeking some method of escape."

Cape May perhaps is better known as a pirate base, but whenever the authorities would crack down on the illicit activity, as they periodically did, the ship captains would disperse up and down the coast, taking advantage of the abundant hiding places.

Occasionally raiding the surrounding farms and villages for provisions, more typically they spent their newly gained wealth locally, purchasing goods and services. Thus by some accounts, not only were they tolerated but also encouraged in their rogue lifestyle.

Ocean Towne's popularity with the pirate community ebbed and flowed with the fortunes of Spain. By the mid-1700s as the Spanish Main's looting of treasures from South America subsided, so did the pirating activity along New Jersey.

But according to legend, they left behind treasure...buried treasure!

Captain Kidd's tale of adventure and betrayal has intrigued treasure hunters for centuries. Reportedly, he hid much of his pirated treasure in a number of locations along the New Jersey coast, from Cape May to Sandy Hook. He admitted as much

> Captain Kidd's Epitaph
> Reader, near this Tomb don't stand
> Without some Essence in thy Hand;
> For here Kidd's stinking Corpse does lie,
> The Scent of which may thee infect. . .

when bargaining for his life before England put him to the hangman's noose and left his tarred and lifeless body dangling over the Thames River as a reminder to other would-be pirates.

Whether the stories of buried treasure are true, the legends concerning their methods for protecting the treasure are frightening. One legend reveals Captain Kidd beheading a fellow pirate and leaving it with his buried treasure. Another has him killing a crewman, and then laying the body across the treasure chest to protect it from treasure hunters. Supposedly, the conspirators made a pact with the dead pirate whereby only three people standing silently in a triangle around the buried treasure under the light of a full moon could dig up the treasure; otherwise, the ghost of the dead pirate would return and avenge the theft of the treasure.

The notorious Blackbeard is said to have buried treasure in New Jersey just as ruthlessly. After his men dug a deep pit to hold the treasure chests, he demanded to know, "Who'll guard this wealth?" When a naïve shipmate volunteered for the job, Blackbeard shot him and his black dog, then buried both of them standing upright in the pit

> Black Shuck: ...a fearsome spectral dog roaming coastal areas at night... an all-black creature about the size of a calf. He has large eyes that glow yellow, red or green as if on fire. Sometimes he is one-eyed... Often, he is headless, yet his eyes ... glow in the dark. He may wear a collar of chains that rattle as he moves...On stormy nights, Black Shuck's bone-chilling howls can be heard rising above the wind. His feet make no sounds and leave no prints, but travelers feel his icy breath upon their necks.
> - British Folklore

to guard the treasure. Legend has it that the apparition of a big black dog can be seen on dark and stormy nights roaming the woods where the treasure is buried.

Perhaps the most intriguing pirate connection to Ocean City is that of "Calico" Jack Rackham and the legendary female pirates Anne Bonny and Mary Read. The legend is told in the 1945 Hollywood movie "The Spanish Main," and their embellished story is filled with irony, romance, violence, justice and mystery, in that order.

Searching for a new career after being pardoned for piracy by the British Governor, Calico Jack met and courted Anne Bonny in the Bahamas where she waited for her husband to return from...of all things...a pirating expedition. Together they stole a ship, and with a small crew they set sail to raid and plunder on the high seas. From a captured vessel, they took on a new crewmember with a ferocious reputation. The ferocious pirate turned out to be a woman, Mary Read, disguised in men's clothes. But fierce she was, and proving herself to be a valuable accomplice, the trio continued prowling and plundering the shipping lanes along the Atlantic coastline.

Reportedly, for a time, Mary Read operated a shop in Cape May where Calico Jack would go to exchange his stolen loot for money. When colonial authorities became aware of the arrangement, they burned the shop and issued warrants for the arrest of Mary and Jack.

Calico Jack displayed a set of crossed cutlasses rather than bones to pronounce his willingness to fight

The reign of terror on British, French and Spanish ships by Calico Jack and the "Pirate Queens" lasted only a few years. A pirate hunter dispatched by the King's navy captured their ship and crew after a brief but violent fight. Accounts of the capture say that only Anne and Mary put up any resistance as the rest of the crew lay drunk below deck. In a fit of rage, Anne is said to have fired a shot at her shipmates screaming, "If there's a man among ye, ye'll come out and fight like the men ye are thought to be!" Her outburst succeeded only in wounding Calico Jack.

Taken to Jamaica and put on trial, the entire crew received a sentence of death by hanging. Revealing that they were pregnant, Anne and Mary received a stay of execution until their babies could be born. Anne, ruthless to the end, is reported to have said goodbye to her lover, Calico Jack, just before his execution by snarling, "...had ye fought like a man, ye need not have been hanged like a dog!"

The "Pirate Queens" suffered a different fate. Mary Read and her baby died from a fever while still in prison. However, Anne Bonny and her baby disappeared, and no record exists of their fate. Some say her rich father bought her freedom, and she

> Mary Read's response when sentenced:
> "As to hanging, it is no great hardship. For were it not for that, every cowardly fellow would turn pirate and so unfit the sea, that men of courage must starve."

returned to South Carolina. Others say she was secreted to Cape May, changed her name to Mary Pritchard and spent her last years on the sparsely populated island of Peck's Beach.

Could the hermit known as Mary Pritchard, said to be one of the few people to have lived on the island prior to the historically recognized original settler, Parker Miller, possibly have been the famous and notorious female pirate Anne Bonny?

Anne Bonny was born in Ireland, and started life as the illegitimate daughter to a wealthy lawyer, William Cormac, and his household maid, Mary Brennan. The disgraced couple sailed to the Americas for a new start and settled in Charleston, South Carolina, where they ran a successful plantation. As Anne grew up, she developed a fiery spirit and wicked temper. She married James Bonny at a young age but left him and ran off to sea with her new lover, the reformed pirate Jack Rackham.

Attractive, sharp witted and daring, she quickly took to the life of pirating. Proving she could fight as well as any man and willing to do so, she also took to dressing as a man while on-board ship. For a while, Rackham, Bonny and Mary Read, once she joined them, became the scourge of the trade ships operating off the Atlantic coast. The fierce trio's well-earned reputation eventually led to the end of Anne's short but sensational career as a pirate.

Anne Bonny lived a glamorized life of adventure, pillaging and plundering on the high seas. She established a reputation of notoriety and worthiness in a field dominated by men. And then she disappeared from history, never to be heard from again.

When Mary Pritchard died after several solitary years on Peck's Beach, her personal possessions reportedly included family heirlooms and documents from the plantation owned by Anne Bonny's father. Is this proof that Mary Pritchard was actually Anne Bonny? Too many years have passed, perhaps, to conclusively prove that is the case. However, it makes for a compelling mystery... particularly if she brought some of that pirate treasure with her...to Ocean City!

Rachel's Attic

If you see her and I see her...and you hear her and I hear her...then perhaps she exists and why not accept the notion!

That is exactly what Ocean City residents Joe and Peggy Parker and daughter Kerry have done - accepted the odd notion that they share their home with a ghost. Built in 1903, the house blends in nicely with the other fine, well-maintained older homes near the center of town on Central Avenue. Although most people may find it too unsettling, too unreal and too bizarre to admit to such an eccentric idea, the Parkers, nevertheless, are convinced it is so.

Joe first suspected something strange might be lurking in their house after a weird incident shortly after the family moved in. Peggy and Kerry were out shopping, and Joe, home alone, headed out the front door to retrieve an item he had left in the car parked at the curb. He returned to the front door, turned the knob and pushed on the door, moving it only an inch or two before it stopped abruptly, opening no further. Joe tried several times, closing and opening the door, pushing and pushing, and always the same thing happened. It felt as though someone blocked the door from opening, as though some mysterious force pressed on it so he could not get in. After several minutes of struggling with the stubborn door, Joe gave up and went around to the back door, and as he entered the house, the front door sprang open! Nothing barred its path... nothing visible that is.

It did not take long for the rest of the family to have encounters either, and they all agree on what they experienced. Disembodied footsteps crossing the attic in the middle of the night, the misty shimmering figure of a young woman, a cat brushing against their leg before its shadowy likeness scrambled behind the furniture or disappeared through the wall.

The misty white form of a young woman appears so frequently around their home, the family decided to give her a name, so they call her Rachel. They describe her as rather attractive and approximately 25-30 years old. Most of their encounters with Rachel take place in the attic, where she can be heard tramping around or occasionally glimpsed roaming about. To add to the enigma, the attic is the one place in the house that their cat never ventures.

Despite not knowing the true identity of their pretty apparition - or her connection to their house - the Parker's accept her presence, and in an odd way are comfortable with the thought that they have a mysterious guest who finds their attic on Central Avenue a comfortable place to haunt.

> goblins: wandering spirits who attach themselves to households, where they alternately help and plague the residents...attracted to homes that have beautiful children and lots of wine.
> -French Folklore

The first part of this story initially appeared in the local weekly tabloid, *Sandpaper*, in an article written by Debbie Duryee for an October issue devoted to the seasonal reappearance on city streets of witches, goblins and other Halloween enthusiasts. Debbie's search for a "true" ghost story led her to Ocean City's Historical Museum where she met Joe and subsequently visited his haunted house for her story.

However, the rest of our tale may not be as pleasant as Duryee's Halloween article. Maybe the paranormal activity in the Parker home can be explained. Perhaps a clue to Rachel's identity exists in a tragic accident that occurred at a rooming house in the Parker's neighborhood. A rooming house that some say is located next to the Parker's house. According to the newspaper account, it happened near midnight. A young woman fell from the second floor roof and landed on the fence below, breaking her neck. Eyewitnesses confirmed that she accidentally slipped. The newspaper reported nothing more about the tragedy.

Additional details, gleaned from a local tradesman who knew the young lady and her boyfriend at the time, may help explain the haunting of the Parker house. Evidently, the woman, frantic to avoid her jealous boyfriend knocking at the door after having tracked her to the rooming house, climbed out a window onto the steep narrow roof in an attempt to hide from her irate pursuer. The shingles, wet and slick from the moist ocean air, caused her to slip and plunge to her death.

Can the young woman's premature departure from this life be the link to the ghostly activity in the Parker's attic? Some feel the possibility exists, particularly since the description of Rachel eerily resembles that of the unfortunate young lady. But no one is sure that Rachel met with this same fate. No one can say if they are one and the same...but who really knows?

What's happening on Central Avenue?

Boardman's Walk

Chances are that it is impossible to find anyone in New Jersey unfamiliar with the Boardwalk, the magical repository of summer decadence. Ice cream parlors, fudge kitchens and saltwater taffy outlets; surf shops, bikini stores and sunglass huts; amusement rides, video arcades and games of chance. Whether perched along the white sandy beaches of Ocean City, Atlantic City, Wildwood or Seaside Heights, the Boardwalk is a child's playland and a grownup's getaway. Everyone knows the Boardwalk, but few have ever heard of Boardman's Walk.

Enterprising businessmen laid the first boardwalk in Atlantic City in 1870, the brainchild of a hotel owner and a train conductor from Camden, Alexander Boardman. Originally designed to alleviate the problem of guests tracking sand into the hotels and onto the train, the portable wooden sections were known as "Boardman's Walk." Visitors to the booming seaside resort quickly took to the idea, and the timbered walkway became a popular thoroughfare for the Victorian-era vacationers. The next decade saw a permanent structure, referred to by the shortened name Boardwalk, constructed along the beach and lined with new retail shops. Eventually, with the addition of amusement halls and piers, the Boardwalk became a worldwide attraction known as "The Playground of the World."

Ocean City recognized a good thing when it saw it, and the growing Christian resort began laying down a boardwalk of its own in 1883 shortly after development on the island gained momentum. Alexander Boardman also followed to Ocean City, purchasing a parcel on the corner of 11th Street and Central Avenue in 1895.

Now our story breaks from conventional history and diverts to the supernatural. Perhaps coincidence...perhaps overactive imagination...whatever is going on, you be the judge.

At one time, the Boardman family owned real estate in New Jersey and Pennsylvania. Records indicate they occupied a house on Cooper Street in Camden, a corner property on 11th Street in Ocean City, a Victorian-era building in Cape May and an estate in the Pennsylvania Dutch farm country. Three of these properties have ghost stories associated with them...ghost stories that involve a woman dressed in white who seemingly prevents accidents from occurring or perhaps may cause accidents. Some think the same spirit is responsible for the sightings and paranormal incidents that plague these sites to this day.

Boardman's corner in Ocean City is at the center of several ghost stories documented in this book. Their neighbors in the old Milabelle Guest House are haunted by a misty female apparition and by guests who have never left. Former nearby resident Joe Parker reports that a young female specter took up residence in the attic of his home. And just down the block, a female phantom continues her haunting forays both inside and outside the Flanders Hotel.

In Pennsylvania, down an old country road, stands an abandoned house from the late 19th century that Alexander Boardman once owned. A local legend claims that Alex's wife died tragically when someone pushed her down the rear staircase in the kitchen, and from that moment she has haunted the old farmhouse. They call her Lizzie, and she continues to roam not only the old homestead but also the surrounding field and roadway.

Auto accidents are said to occur frequently on the solitary stretch of road running by the house. Drivers veer off into the fields and trees when a woman, dressed in white, suddenly appears in the beam of their headlights. During October, the house is open to the public as a Halloween fright-house, and reports

> phantom hitchhiker: a girl or woman, sometimes in distress...spotted late at night, standing by the side of a lonely stretch of road...or sometimes looming up suddenly in the headlights...often dressed in white.
> –American folklore

of encounters with the enigmatic poltergeist are common. She appears periodically on the steps of her untimely death and at times outside in the overgrown yard. Reportedly, Lizzie is rather fussy about the people she prefers to have in her former home. Those with evil intentions or sinister morals are harassed by her and usually end up with bad luck or in unexplainable accidents. A young girl wantonly causing damage inside the house shortly thereafter wrecked her car. A man known to deceive and con his employers fell down the same staircase where Lizzie had her "accident" breaking his thumb. And a businessman intent on scamming his way to some unearned income found himself in need of a new vehicle when his truck ended up in the deep culvert opposite the house.

Cape May is a town inundated with ghost stories, and a beautiful 19th century Victorian-style guesthouse, once owned by the Boardman family, since moved and improbably named the "Merry Widow," is reportedly the home to a female spirit that can sometimes be glimpsed roaming the halls of the grand structure.

Of course the chance that the same vengeful "lady in white" could possibly haunt these widely separated properties is unlikely - just one big supernatural coincidence. After all, three different properties owned at one time by the same family, separated by more than a hundred miles and scores of communities,

The enigmatic grave

spanning two states, would more likely be haunted by three totally unrelated spirits. Never mind the fact that a woman in white is seen in all three places. There are hundreds of disappearing white phantoms in ghost stories around the world. No matter that Alex's wife reportedly died prematurely and under suspicious circumstances. As a matter of fact, it is not all that uncommon to have a member of the family buried somewhere other than in the family plot, as is the case with Alex. But it sure makes you wonder what the *hex* going on! What do you think?

Halloween

Ocean City's Halloween parade has existed since the early part of the 20th century. But the scarier elements of the holiday occur elsewhere as this October newspaper headline from the 1930's portrays:

Dancing Spirits?

Restless Spirit

"*Restless Spirit*"- a great name for a ghost story and also the name of the book and record (yes record!) shop located on 8th Street between Central and Wesley Avenues. And whether the name refers to a ghost story, a record shop or the wanderlust of human nature - there is no question of restless spirits cavorting in the fittingly named shop in Ocean City.

One of the island's newer retail outlets, The Restless Spirit offers an eclectic collection of vinyl records, used books and musical instruments. When Dave, a long-time Ocean City resident, opened this unique shop of hard-to-find items, he also opened the door to a story of dancing ghosts and the mystery of a building and its unknown past.

Dave and his coworkers first noticed the noise coming from upstairs while renovating the first floor area where the shop is located. During the long days and nights of painting, papering and arranging merchandise in preparation for the grand opening, the unmistakable sound of footsteps on the second floor were a frequent companion. The area upstairs remained unoccupied after a fire damaged the space several years earlier, and they should not have heard the sound of rhythmic footsteps.

Several trips up the back steps to investigate revealed nothing and no one. However, they soon realized the impossibility of what they were hearing. The layout of the walls and doorways upstairs would prevent the footsteps from taking the direction they seemed to be traveling!

Upstairs dance hall?

Not much is known about the building's history or its former occupants, except for the seamstress who lived upstairs for many years. She also operated a shop on the first floor in another part of the building. A "reading" of the building by a local psychic identified a cold spot near the old kitchen upstairs and the faint presence of something in the foyer, but little else. Dave heard from a neighboring shop owner that at one time, decades ago, a dance studio operated upstairs, providing the only clue to what might be the source of the mysterious sound effects.

The story of the ghostly dancing footsteps at Restless Spirit is one of the ghost stories told on the *Ghost Tour of Ocean City*. Unable to document the existence of the dance hall, the Restless Spirit story is told as a *"we heard"*-type story based on passing comments from a few local residents. However, the dance studio theory gained support when a customer on the evening tour reacted oddly while listening to the haunted tale of the Restless Spirit.

> **The Devil Went Down to Jersey**
>
> According to a "piney" legend, "Fiddler Sammy Buck" was the greatest dancer and fiddler in South Jersey. In a match with the Devil, Sammy lost a dance contest but saved his soul when he beat the Devil in a fiddle contest by playing a tune the Devil had never heard before.

The woman became visibly agitated when she heard that the upper floor possibly served as an old dance hall. As the tour guide continued the story – trying to paint the image of long ago dancers waltzing gracefully across the floor – the woman's discomfort increased. When the story concluded, the guide discretely asked her if she felt ok and apologized for upsetting her. The woman's reply provided perhaps the best clue to date on the haunting of the Restless Spirit.

As she chuckled nervously, she shared her story that night, describing the reason why the tale of the Restless Spirit upset her. The woman's family lived in town for many years, and her aged father had recently passed away after residing in a nursing home for several years, afflicted with dementia. She continued with the sad description of his disability – unable to recall anything short term, but remembering things from his long ago past. In his final weeks, he kept insisting that he wanted to go dancing. One particular day he demanded they take him to the dance hall – the dance hall on 8th Street. The family despairingly thought his disease had finally gotten the best of him, for they had never heard of a dance hall on 8th Street where their loved one wished to dance in his last days. As she stood there looking up at the second floor of the building, she wondered whether her father had once danced in the building... *we wonder if he still does!*

Moonlight Ghosts

Unknown to many, nature is the source of ghosts that live on the beaches of Ocean City. Appearing mainly at night, these translucent whitish creatures can also be glimpsed during the day as they scurry back and forth to the surf. They are "ghost crabs," two-inch spider-like crustaceans that live in holes along the beach.

Their burrows exist several feet below the surface and are easily identified by the approximately one-inch entrance hole visible just beyond the high tide line. With 360 degree rotating periscope-like eyes and oversize pinchers, they are the perfect companions for a moonlight stroll on the beach!

Buried in the sand at 16th Street?

Curse of the Buddha

A stormy night...
A drunken crew...
A smuggled treasure...
...cursed by a "Golden Buddha?"

A book on Ocean City just would not be complete without a tale about the Sindia, the 19th century sailing vessel that wrecked on the beach one fateful night more than 100 years ago.

The details and conjecture concerning the purpose of the Sindia's final voyage, and her tragic demise on December 15, 1901, have fascinated generations of Ocean City natives and visitors alike. The generally accepted story is well documented. The Sindia, returning to New York from a routine trading mission to Asia, wrecked on the Ocean City beach during a violent storm. However, from the moment it appeared that wintry December morning, mired in the unrelenting grasp of the sand, rumors and hearsay have swirled about.

Several articles published over the decades point to controversial and uncorroborated reasons for the voyage as well as the wreck. Suggesting, perhaps, a moneyed conspiracy connected to the Rockefeller fortune, an inept

and drunken crew, and a hex, emanating from a fearsome icon plundered from China. More than merely a stranded trading ship lolled on the sand that cold wintry morning...a mystery, perhaps reaching to the other side of the world, lay entombed in her...a mystery the passage of time would only enhance.

> funayuhrei: a ghost ship that travels silently at night or in thick fog. It appears suddenly without sound or lights. Meeting one on the sea is fatal. The appearance...will cause a ship to start to turn violently in circles and then sink. The doomed ship then becomes a funayuhrei itself. As for the victims, if they are lucky, they drown. If they are unlucky, they might be captured, tortured and eaten by the isohime, a giant, fantastical mermaid that likes to catch the survivors of sinking ships.
>
> –Japanese Folklore

In a 1906 newspaper article on the disaster, tantalizing details surfaced: "It became apparent that the Sindia was carrying undocumented cargo...when divers brought up items that were not listed on the ship's manifest. The designs and individual markings suggested Chinese origin, rather than Japanese, and included a pair of porcelain Chinese Foo dogs – each weighing over 200 pounds – plus 12 bronze jardinières and a four-foot-high cloisonné vase."

A 1929 newspaper account gave a more sensational and provocative account: "The wreck of the mysterious old bark, Sindia...Named for a savage East India chieftain...purchased...by one of the wealthiest corporations on the globe, and then steered from her course by fate and landed on the sands of Jersey with a million dollar cargo, the Sindia presents the thrill-hunter with a kaleidoscope array of sensations. Deep down in the hold of the ship...is a venerable and perhaps, a terrible Chinese god...which has been unable to extricate itself from the wreck...there is an attraction...that is far more weird and harder to understand than life itself."

From the 1961 essay "Did A Strange Curse Sink The Sindia?" by William McMahon, we get more tantalizing tidbits to arouse the imagination: "Was it another curse, stemming from the hidden jungle shrines of a mysterious land that sent a four-masted bargue flying over reefs that even a small boat could not manage, to be thrown onto the beach....Jack Morely...who was the lookout that fatal night had an answer. 'Look to that 'eathen idol.' On the waterfront of Philadelphia for a long time after the tragedy the inns echoed to weird tales of unearthly sounds in the hold of the Sindia on the final, terrifying night...the hold that carried a two-ton idol of a forbidden sect...having wrecked vengence upon those who would bring it to a land of unbelievers, have the gods whom the idol represented returned it to its original home? The ways of the Orient are not our ways and the forces which have guided it through thousands of years are many times unexplainable...Her skipper...Capt. McKenzie was a Christian man and protested taking the two-ton monster aboard...'There will no good come of it.' He instructed that the idol be placed below and firmly fastened. 'I want none of it,' he told his mate. 'I'm a God-fearing man and I don't like the heathen images aboard my ship.'...at one point of the voyage there was a hush-hush movement to throw the thing overboard...the voyage continued with no mishaps... Then something happened. A giant swell threw her hard over...She seemed to have a mind of her own and failed to answer the steersman...nothing could stop the Sindia's mad race...and she finally grounded deep in the sand at 17th street...If the idol is still in the sands guarding its treasures does it hold a curse for anyone who disturbs it? Did its curse wreck McKenzie and the Sindia?"

On a 2001 tour at the Ocean City Historical Museum, a splendid repository of Sindia relics, the mystique and intrigue continued, as told by the museum's tour guide: "Legend says that sailors on the Sindia stole a golden Buddha from the Orient shortly before returning to the United States. They smuggled it on board and hid it below the deck wrapped in tarps...when the Sindia ran aground, and subsequently its valuable load of china, silks and other treasures were salvaged, the golden Buddha was unaccounted for. However, many items, not listed on the ships manifest and believed to be from China, were salvaged, which is the basis of the legend...that also says the bottom-most hold of the ship has never been accessed. In later years a salvage team, in an attempt to reach that hold, cut a hole into the submerged vessel...and just as a diver was about to enter, a storm blew up and pushed the salvage boat out into the ocean. When they finally pulled the diver from the wreck he was panicked...near a nervous

> sea gull: In the lore of Irish fisherman, sea gulls embody the souls of drowning victims.
>
> -Irish Folklore

breakdown...claiming it was haunted and he would never go in again. Legend has it that no one has!"

So, did the abducted Buddha curse the Sindia, causing her to run ashore and lose her cargo, therefore preventing the recovery of her looted treasure? Some think so. But did the curse extend to Ocean City and Captain MacKenzie, too? Perhaps...for despite the brutal conditions present during the grounding - a savage storm in pitch-black darkness on a bitterly cold night - no deaths occurred. However, coincidently, on that very same morning, Ocean City's pioneer resident, Parker Miller, took sick and never recovered, dying a week later. Oddly enough, he had constructed his house from the remains of another ship that had wrecked on the Ocean City beach. And it is said that the Sindia's captain, Allan MacKenzie, died of a broken heart shortly after standing trial for the disaster, where he was found guilty of "carelessness."

For those not familiar with the details of the disaster and the history of the Sindia, a brief summary follows:

The Sindia was a grand four-masted steel ship built in 1887 in Belfast, Ireland by Harland & Wolf, the same company that built the ill-fated Titanic.

Used primarily for East Indian and Asian trade, she had

THE "SINDIA" —1901

sailed with no trouble for over 200,000 miles around the globe. In 1900, Standard Oil Company, owned by John D. Rockefeller, purchased her for $200,000. She was huge – 329 feet long and 45 feet wide. Her fateful voyage began in Bayonne, NJ, where she was loaded with case oil. Her destination was Shanghai, China, then Kobe, Japan to pick up her load to bring to New York. Her manifest indicated she was loaded with cargo that included matting, manganese ore, Oriental curios and china.

The Sindia sailed shortly after the outbreak of the Boxer Rebellion in China where smuggling of fine art and religious artifacts flourished. While at port, supposedly her crew smuggled aboard artifacts from looted Buddhist temples, including the statue of a golden Buddha. Captain Allan MacKenzie brought the Sindia safely across the Pacific, around the tip of Cape Horn crossing the Atlantic to the coast of New Jersey – some 10,000 miles. He was a master in his art, and seamen claimed, "His satanic majesty never sent a gale that did not turn in favor of MacKenzie." The ship hugged the shore as it approached New York City; many say too closely in such a storm. There were reports of drinking on board, while some say the soundings were not checked often enough. Some say they were hugging the shoreline for a reason. The coast of New Jersey, with its myriad bays and inlets, served for hundreds of years as a haven for smugglers and pirates. Perhaps some of the cargo was destined for Ocean City after all.

With waves and wind pummeling her deeper and deeper into the sand, the Sindia became lodged on two prior wrecks in the area between 16th and 17th Streets, becoming a fixture on the beach and Ocean City's greatest legend. The Ocean City Life Saving Station rescued all hands on board. Some of her cargo was salvaged and sold, and much of it ended up in the homes and shops on the island. Many years later, a sailor, who was on the Sindia that fateful morning, claimed that the Buddha was the first thing off the stranded ship.

Numerous salvage expeditions have been attempted since - none completely successful. As recently as 1999, a salvage company explored the possibility of making another recovery attempt, but nothing has come of it to date.

Is it any wonder that the notoriety of buried treasure cursed by a mystical deity, continues to keep the long ago incident of the Sindia's grounding in the forefront of Ocean City's history? Perhaps someday we will discover what really resides in the bottom hold of the Sindia buried beneath the sand off Ocean City. But after more than a century of intrigue, the mystery remains, and she continues to hold her secrets...beckoning secrets...buried with her, and perhaps, guarded by a golden Buddha!

Walter Kennedy, a visitor to Ocean City, wrote this poem in 1929 after viewing the wreck while strolling on the boardwalk. *But despite the title, the Sindia has yet to be forgotten!*

"FORGOTTEN"

Far from my own Nippon,
Far from the shadows of the sacred Fugi,
Lie my bones, rottening
On the shores of a people
Not of me.

The icy gales of winter
And the gentle winds of summer,
As they moan and sigh through my riggings,
Sing a requiem for me.

Thus have the Fates decreed:
Pitiless tides and shifting sands
Will soon cover me
From the sight of man,
A forgotten ship.

The Cedar Tree Shrine

Standing lost among the sand dunes of Cedar Beach on the southern tip of Ocean City, a lonely cedar tree harbors a secret. Hidden high in its branches are several perplexing objects - a wooden cross adorned with a seashell ornament and a conch shell wrapped in colorful ribbon. What other mysteries lay concealed in the maze of trails at this desolate end of the island?

Death Alley

The bustling summer sounds of Ocean City mix together as they echo across the seaside resort. Generated by throngs of vacationers, sun worshippers and fishermen; accentuated by the pounding ocean surf and clanking boardwalk amusements; the crowd's distorted jabbering caroms against the walls of the downtown buildings as it crosses the island in a jumble of noise. Some people say that if you listen closely, you may also hear the fury of a violent and desperate struggle in those echoes, perhaps punctuated by gunshots and running footsteps!

One area in particular seems prone to the clamoring din. Located in the center of town, the alleyway from 8th to 9th Streets between Asbury and Central Avenues bears a history of tragedy that might explain the unusual sounds that are known to haunt the area. The alley is the site of a cold-blooded killing perpetrated some 70 years ago that was reportedly Ocean City's first murder, a shocking senseless death that stunned the city.

The heavily used alley running through the heart of the business district hummed with activity back in 1933. One of the City's most popular establishments, Murphy's Five and Ten Cent Store, stood on the corner of 8th Street and Asbury Avenue in the Bourse Building; the six-story bank building towered on the opposite corner, and the Post Office sat on 8th Street next to the alley.

And the *alley* is the place where Larry Imbesi, a local man, had an unfortunate encounter with a disturbed drifter who went by the name of George Brown. That *alley* became the scene of a tragic struggle between a young man in his prime and a hardened criminal who had no sanctity for human life.

Over 100 miles of roads, streets, avenues and alleys crisscross the seven-mile-long island of Ocean City from north to south and bay to ocean. Many of the alleys date from an era prior to indoor plumbing, when privies, or outhouses, were located at the back of the property near the alleyway. This placement served several purposes. Unpleasant odors were removed from the general living quarters, and it provided easy access for pumping the contents for disposal. Today, the alleys still serve a useful purpose, primarily for deliveries to businesses and for disposal of trash. Motorists, bicyclists and pedestrians also find the alleys useful as shortcuts while navigating the busy summer streets.

Larry graduated from Ocean City High School, attended dentistry school and planned to pursue a law degree. He spent his summers working in Ocean City, several of those for the Post Office.

An account of the fateful day by the Ocean City Daily newspaper begins with a city police officer's encounter with a "rum crazed panhandler" on the street corner outside Murphy's store. When the stranger, reported to be George Brown, entered Murphy's store, the officer followed. Brown saw the policeman following, and he headed out the side door onto 8th Street where the officer quickly caught up to him. Brown reacted unexpectedly, pulling a revolver from inside a bag he carried. The officer's own quick reaction enabled him to knock the gun upward just as Brown pulled the trigger, and fortunately for the officer, the bullet whizzed over his head. Immediately, Brown dashed across 8th Street and scrambled down the alley between the bank building and the Post Office, firing shots back at the pursuing police officer.

Call it bad luck or call it misfortune. As the fleeing Brown ducked behind the Post Office, Larry Imbesi and a coworker, Maurice Johnson, emerged from a back door of the building. Caught unsuspectingly in the dangerous drama playing itself out, the two postal employees became entangled with the desperate criminal. They wrestled Brown to the ground, but intent on making his escape, the panicked desperado struggled fiercely, and at some point during the fray, he squeezed off several shots, hitting both men. They lay gravely wounded in the back alley of the Post Office; Larry shot in the stomach and Maurice hit several times. The commotion brought help from the nearby police station, and following a short pursuit down Asbury Avenue, the officers cornered Brown where he surrendered, but only after running out of bullets.

Larry and his coworker were rushed to the hospital, but for Larry the struggle had ended. He died shortly thereafter. Maurice, however, recovered after a long recuperation period in the hospital. According to Maurice, who adamantly claimed that Larry saved his life in the scuffle with Brown, Larry died a hero.

George Brown received a speedy trial and spent the remaining years of his life in jail after being found guilty of the murder of Larry Imbesi.

Traumatized by the young man's murder, it took many years for the genteel city to forget the alarming incident.

Among the downtown merchants, it became the main topic of discussion for some time, but eventually, the memory of that ill-fated day faded. However, the alley continues as a place of bizarre tragedies.

Just a short distance down the alley, City Hall employees tell the story of an accident that claimed the life of a contractor while refurbishing their building. From the back roof of City Hall, the man fell, hitting electrical wires that in turn came in contact with the outside wall. The plaster on the inside wall exploded, exposing the metal beam and causing it to look as though struck by lightening. The unlucky worker died in the alley behind City Hall. His family came from Ireland to retrieve his body for burial in his native land.

In the parking lot next to the alley, where the Post Office once stood, where Larry Imbesi fought for his life, an incident occurred that no one really wants to talk about. A well-known and fondly remembered city resident committed suicide there. Evidently, he suffered from a terminal illness and shot himself while sitting in his car, and the note he left behind stated that he chose the location because of its convenience to the funeral parlor on Central Avenue.

What could be causing the unusual number of tragedies along this one stretch of alley? Does a vortex of negative energy exist? Is it a *"something evil this way comes"* syndrome?

Reports of paranormal activity occurring in the immediate area do exist. Current tenants in the Bourse Building, where Murphy's Five and Ten once operated, claim to have encountered an

> Excerpt from
> "Something Evil This Way Comes"
> by Franklin Lee Mallory
>
> Something evil this way comes
> Upon a breeze in darkness ride
> The darkened spirits growl and whine
>
> Standing hair, crawling skin
> A feeling spawns from within...

invisible presence near the rear of the building. But they sense a playful, teasing nature particularly with women. An out of town newspaper man, a native of Ocean City, heard that a ghost supposedly haunts the upper floors of the old bank building- the ghost of a man that hung himself years ago.

Nearby residents and shopkeepers say that loud sounds coming from the alley are common. Some say that they occasionally hear running footsteps, angry shouts, and sharp bangs that could pass as gunshots. Is it, as some believe, the tragedy from 1933 playing out over and over again? Does Larry return in a never-ending attempt to flee from his unexpected fate? Or is it just the noise from the nearby hustle-bustle of the shopping district and the sound of the summer crowd echoing in the alley?

The Island in 1925

SENIOR
STUDIO

Ghost Town

Ocean City is a ghost town. Literally. On an island crammed from ocean to bay with dwellings of every kind, you can drive or walk the deserted lonely streets for the greater part of nine months and barely see a soul.

As with most summer resorts at the Jersey shore, the streets of Ocean City are jammed, and almost every available room is taken during June, July and August. The rest of the year the island takes on an eerie, unsettling aura of abandonment for those left behind. But just because everyone is gone does not mean the tightly locked and battened down buildings are necessarily empty. Ghost stories are common all over Ocean City, and as the following tales suggest, the island is well populated with non-seasonal guests who have no desire leave.

Two young ladies claim that their great-grandfather haunts the family home on Stenton Place. He appears in the lower bedroom, moves furniture around and can be detected by the cold spot that moves through the room. One of the girls sensed him sitting next to her on the bed stroking her arm. Their great-grandmother, still alive at 94, has lived in the house since the 1940s. Evidently, her husband never wanted to leave the island, and since there is not a single cemetery in Ocean City, she buried his ashes in the backyard.

Tom tells the story of a house named the Lonely Mermaid on Central Avenue near 1st Street. He sees flashes of light and hears footsteps in an

> domovik: a household spirit that resides in every home...the ancestral founder of the family, and moves with it from house to house...portrayed as an old man with a gray beard, ... lives behind the stove... watches over family members... if family members displease him, he makes poltergeist-like noise disturbances. His harshest punishment is to burn down the house... other type of domoviks...the bannik, who lives in the bathroom...the ovinnik, who lives in the kitchen.
>
> -Russian Folklore

unused room next to the master bedroom. He and his wife named the phantom stalker George after the man who owned the house previously. Tom also experienced a blinding flash of light, "like the mark of Zorro," as he opened the sliding glass door one night after returning home from working the "graveyard" shift. While talking to his neighbor, he mentioned the odd footsteps and flashes of light and found out that George died in the house of a heart attack after shoveling snow.

Vince, a descendant of the Ocean City founding family of Lakes, currently lives at 3rd and Ocean where man's best friend keeps him company - a faithful ghost dog. He hears the phantom pet scrambling up and down the staircase and in other parts of the house as well.

A woman from Allentown who spends almost every summer vacation in Ocean City swears that a house on a corner of Brighton Place is haunted. The incident happened almost 20 years ago when she accompanied her girlfriend's family to the shore. Only 15 years old at the time, she felt uncomfortable the moment they pulled into the driveway but did not know why. That night she could not sleep and heard doors constantly opening and closing. At about 4:00 a.m. she glanced at the clock, and as she rolled over, a woman appeared in the doorway. Staring at the figure dressed in a nightgown and carrying a flower, she realized that with its long dark hair, the illusory visitor eerily resembled *her*...except it had no face. The

> Faceless Gray Man:
> ...legend of an apparition of a gray man with no face who appears just before hurricanes strike...
> -Carolina Coast Folklore

vision disappeared, and she fell sound asleep. At the breakfast table the next morning, her girlfriend's mother mentioned that she saw her walking around in a long nightgown during the night. When she explained that she slept in an orange t-shirt and panties and it could not have been her, they all spent that night sleeping in the same room.

In the building next to Jim Penland's place at 7th and Asbury, Jim reports small, sparkling blue lights that grow to the size of dinner plates. His frequent companion, a long-hair Mexican Chihuahua that goes by the name Tootsie, also sees the phenomena and runs under the couch to hide. This makes sense since these dogs are known

Jim & Tootsie

to be psychic and, according to Jim, are carried in neck pouches by some in Mexico to ward off evil spirits.

Josh, a local young man, claims his home on Mercer Place by the bay is haunted by his mother's friend. He thinks the female spirit seeks retribution for her death, a murder made to look like a suicide.

On the wonderfully spooky 600 block of Central Avenue a man claims a vanishing little girl awakens him from a deep sleep. Her name is Anna, and she asks to go to the bathroom. When he tells her to go ahead and go, she always replies, "But I'm not allowed outside after dark," and then she mysteriously disappears. He thinks that perhaps his visitor is referring to the outhouse that once stood out back. The nocturnally disturbed man is unsure of the identity of the unsettling little girl, but his house is next to a building that at one time functioned as a funeral parlor formerly owned by the Lake family.

A longtime self-proclaimed "shoobie" is certain a spiritual spirit haunts the Music Pier. As she entered the south side of the pier through the iron gates on an unusually slow day on the boardwalk, the figure of a nun appeared. The opaque misty form

> phantom nuns: ghosts allegedly belonging to women of the church...they haunt religious buildings or buildings built on the former site of religious institutions.
> – English Folklore

sported a large habit similar to the type worn by the nuns on the show the "Flying Nun." She wondered whether the "glimmering nun" at one time attended a religious ceremony held at the Music Pier.

Marc, a lifetime resident, suspects that a local author who committed suicide by hanging may haunt an apartment near Asbury and 9th. When Marc lived in the apartment strange eerie noises could be heard coming from the closet, and when his band practiced there, they always had trouble with their heretofore trouble-free amplifiers.

An old Native American is said to haunt the area of 9th and Wesley. According to Kim, his granddaughter, he came from a Cherokee reservation in Delaware and holds the distinction of being the first Native American to permanently live on the island.

Yet another story from the Flanders involves six young people who were staying at the hotel. After taking the Ghost Tour, they went back to the hotel to check out the painted mural of Emily, and all six claim to have seen her standing in front of her picture.

According to Louise, a local resident, the benevolent spirit of the former owner resides in a house on 12th Street near the bay. She believes that he saved her from injury as she tumbled down a flight of steps in the house. Louise unexpectedly felt a firm hand pressing on her chest, holding her up as she fell unhurt to the bottom.

An old man dressed in a blue shirt who vanishes into thin air is said to visit a well-established gift shop on the Boardwalk near 13th Street. Sometimes the old gent is dressed like a sea captain and is accompanied by a female companion. He seems to be a very sociable spirit and reportedly is spotted in the wintertime hanging out on the rooftop porch of a nearby hotel having a good time with other ghost guests.

> bucca-boo: a sea spirit that lives among fishermen, helping them, or plaguing them when not [appeased]... To stay in the good graces of bucca-boos, fishermen traditionally leave a fish from their catch on the sand. They also toss a piece of bread over their left shoulder and spill a little bit of their beer on the ground.
>
> -Cornish Folklore

Bill, an old-time islander now living in a condo on the bay, remembered a weird episode back in the 1960s in a summer rental home on the lagoon near 18th Street. As usual for a summer Friday night, his 16-year-old daughter cruised the Boardwalk until about 11:00. When she returned, Bill and his wife had already retired for the evening. As she entered the kitchen, the sound of their

100-pound Airedale Terrier crying and whimpering came from under the table. She felt a cold breeze, and out of nowhere a woman's voice demanded, "What are you doing here?" With that, both she and the dog ran into her parent's room and jumped in bed with them. But that did not end the strange doings that made him remember that weekend some 40 years later. The next evening, they had some friends over to enjoy a few beers and watch the Phillies on television. As they relaxed, the back door suddenly opened and slammed shut on its own. Later, the owner admitted to having had similar experiences and attributed it to his dead mother who never wanted to leave the island.

The ghost of a TV character look-alike may share a home with husband and wife Polly and Tom on 22nd Street. Built in 1959, a woman passed away inside the house in 1965. Evidently, a strong resemblance exists between the ghostly visitor, who shares their dreams and is rather noisy around the house, the woman who died and Al Bundy's wife from the show "Married...with Children."

From a non-believer comes a story from the 2600 block of Wesley where a woman, denying any belief in the supernatural, nevertheless speaks of her own encounters with the netherworld. In her house, built in the 1940s by a wealthy couple from Vineland, she periodically catches a glimpse of a passing figure. Of the original owners, the husband died, and a short time later, his wife suffered from senility. The next owners were afflicted with the same fate. The wife survived the husband, but she too "went senile." The question of whether the non-believer's husband still walked the earth did not arise.

Near 32nd Street and the bay, the spirit of a crazy widowed woman, who committed suicide by walking into a salt pond and drowning herself, is seen walking the bayside

> rusalka: ...the spirit of a maiden who drowns by accident or by force and becomes a ghost who haunts the spot where she died...
> -Russian Folklore

streets. According to a newspaper report, the disturbed woman had tried unsuccessfully to end her life several times after her husband died before she finally took her last swim.

So despite the false impression of a deserted island portrayed by empty streets most of the year, Ocean City is really quite lively year round, even though the activity may come from those who have no intention of leaving...dead or alive.

GHOST STORIES OF OCEAN CITY, NJ

Acknowledgements

Editor: Alanna Lynne Reeser

Cain, Tim. *Peck's Beach: A Pictorial History of Ocean City, New Jersey*
Guiley, RoseMary Ellen. *The Encyclopedia of Ghosts and Spirits*
Lee, Harold. *A History of Ocean City New Jersey, Ocean City Memories*
Luff, William. *The Story of the Ocean City Tabernacle*
Mallory, Franklin Lee. "Something Evil This Way Comes"
McCloy, James & Miller Jr., Ray. *The Jersey Devil*
McMahon, William. *Pine Barrens Legends & Lore*
McPhee, John. *The Pine Barrens*
Ogden, Tom. *The Complete Idiot's Guide to Ghosts & Hauntings*
Voss, J. Ellis. *Ocean City: An Ecological Analysis of a Satellite Community*

Atlantic City Press
Atlantic City Historical Society
Cape May County Clerk's Office
Flanders Hotel
Ocean City Historical Museum
Ocean City Public Library
Ocean City Sentinel
Oyster Creek Inn
Senior Studio
The Sandpaper
www.flyvision.org
www.ghosttour.com

John Boardman
Joe Clark
Ed & Barb DeMarco
Debbie Duryee
John Loeper
Linda Long

John Moore
Ed Nardo
Jim Penland
Dave Swift
Jeanne Swift
Tony Troy